the English Rose

DAVID AUSTIN

the English Rose

DAVID AUSTIN

conran
OCTOPUS

Commissioning Editor Stuart Cooper
Editors Paula Hardy, Sarah Sears
Art Editor Isabel de Cordova
Picture Research Clare Taylor
Production Amanda Sneddon

First published in 1998 by
Conran Octopus Limited
37 Shelton Street, London WC2H 9HN

British Library Cataloguing-in-Publication
Data. A catalogue record for this book is
available from the British Library

ISBN 1 84091 027 5
Printed in China

CONTENTS

introduction

I started breeding roses in the early 1950s, although it was not until 1965 that I became a professional nurseryman and founded David Austin Roses. I began with a small collection of Hybrid Teas and Floribundas, but for some reason I found these unsatisfactory. They seemed to me to be too harsh in colour and they lacked charm and grace. Soon afterwards, I chanced upon George Bunyard's catalogue of Old Roses. George Bunyard was a nurseryman in Kent who gathered together the first commercial collection of Old Roses. The black-and-white photographs in this catalogue made me realize that there were better roses to be had than many of the examples of that time, and I duly sent away for a small number of bushes.

The main problem with Old Roses is that they flower only once in a season, whereas Modern Roses flower throughout the summer. They also have a very limited colour range, being restricted to shades of white, pink and purple. There were few true crimsons until the arrival of the Hybrid Perpetual Rose, and there are no yellow roses outside the Tea Roses, which are very difficult to grow. However, they do have a delicious fragrance and, even more importantly, they possess a charm and beauty that I could not find among other roses of the time.

A beautiful arrangement of English Rose Bow Bells, with lavender, violas and other flowers.

Left Two beautiful Old Roses – 'La Ville de Bruxelles' and 'Charles de Mills' – typical of those used in the development of English Roses.
Right A Shropshire Lad – a large, strong-growing English Rose, well suited to the back of the border.

It therefore occurred to me that it might be possible, by means of hybridization, to combine the beauty and the fragrance of the Old Roses with the practical qualities of the Modern Roses. The result, after some 50 years of work, is what are now known as English Roses. The development of these roses has involved the raising of many hundreds of thousands of seedlings from which, after rigorous selection, I have chosen almost 100 new English roses. We are continuing to work on these roses on an even larger scale today, and hope to make further improvements as time goes by.

The nature of English Roses

English Roses are small shrubs, usually with bushy, branching growth, although this can vary greatly. Some may have gracefully arching growth; others have tall, almost columnar growth. They may be small or quite large and their foliage – which is an attraction in itself, particularly early in the year – can vary considerably.

The flowers, which can be single or semi-double, also vary between the different roses. The most usual shape is that of a rosette, often tightly packed with petals. Others may be cupped in shape, either deeply or shallowly, more

Above English Roses can look beautiful even when placed casually, after picking, into a bucket. Somehow, they seem to have a way of arranging themselves to beautiful effect.

like a saucer. These cups may be filled with small petals, or they may show the golden stamens within, or the petals may turn back to form a domed flower. In addition, there are variations of all these shapes.

Scent is another major attribute among English Roses, being almost as important as the appearance of the flower. It is not an exaggeration to say that they are more fragrant than any other class of rose. The fragrances vary widely from the true Old Rose fragrance and the Tea Rose fragrance to a variety of fruity scents; there are also some spicy scents, which are often reminiscent of myrrh. We have made an extensive (and pleasurable) study of these scents and it is possible to note, in the background, further tints such as that of raspberry, fresh apples or cucumber.

Our aim in the development of English Roses is variety – of size, flower, foliage, colour and scent. As roses are the most widely grown of all plants, nothing could be worse in a garden than to see the same type repeated over and over again.

English Roses in the garden

English Roses associate well with other flowers and can be used to excellent effect in mixed borders – something that cannot be said for most Hybrid Teas and Floribundas. The soft colours never clash with those of other plants and their natural growth is also an asset. A border made up of English Roses, perhaps with Old Roses and other Modern Shrub Roses mixed in, can be a source of great interest and pleasure throughout the summer. Neither are they out of place in the conventional rose bed, but in this case it would be better to choose some of the shorter ones. Then there is the rose garden itself, which must be the ideal choice for every rose lover. This is, of course, dependent upon having sufficient space and, perhaps, time and resources. The rose garden has traditionally been planted exclusively with Modern Hybrid Teas and Floribundas: Old Roses and many other Shrub Roses have always had too short a flowering period – perhaps just two or three weeks – to be considered for this purpose. With the arrival of the English Roses, it is now possible to have an 'Old Rose' garden in flower throughout the summer.

Not least among the virtues of English Roses is their value as cut flowers. All those who like to arrange flowers for the house will find English Roses ideal for this purpose. Their soft and agreeable colours blend perfectly to make the most beautiful effects and their scent will fill a room.

abraham darby

A magnificent centrepiece for a border or a flower arrangement. The large, coppery-apricot flowers, shading to soft pink on the outer petals, are held above plentiful, shiny foliage. The flowers are of classic Old Rose shape, deeply cupped and filled with a profusion of petals, and they carry a rich, fruity fragrance. Abraham Darby repeat-flowers throughout the summer and autumn, and makes a vigorous, well-rounded, healthy bush.

H 1.5m (5ft) × W 1.5m (5ft) 1985

ambridge rose

A lovely little rose for the front of the border or the smaller garden. The flowers are a gentle apricot-pink, shading to a beautiful soft pale pink at the edges. Ambridge Rose can also be used in large groups as a bedding rose, where its neat habit and tough constitution make it invaluable. This is a real cottage-garden rose, with a delightful, herby, country-garden fragrance of Old Rose, fennel and myrrh. It was named after and featured in the BBC's long-running serial, *The Archers*.

H 1m (3½ft) x W 75cm (2½ft) 1990

brother cadfael

Named after novelist Ellis Peters' detective hero, the 12th-century Shropshire monk Brother Cadfael, this rose has a medieval splendour, with huge, globe-shaped blooms like paeonies – rich pink, and filled with masses of incurving petals. The flowers look wonderful in the centre of a flower arrangement, and last well both on the bush and as a cut flower, when their deep Old Rose fragrance will scent any room.

H 1.2m (4ft) x W 1m (3½ft) 1990

charles austin

This is a very tall, upright rose, and its abundant foliage is large and modern in appearance. It bears large, fine, cup-shaped blooms much appreciated by flower-arrangers. The flowers come in varying shades of apricot – which fades with time – and they have a strong, fresh fruit fragrance. One of the earlier examples of English Rose, it has proved popular, despite the fact that it does not repeat-flower well and, without severe pruning, can become leggy and ungainly.

H 1.5m (5ft) x W 1m (3½ft) 1973

charles rennie mackintosh

This rose has the tough
constitution and continuous
flowering habit that make
English Roses invaluable. The
scented blooms have large,
cupped outer petals holding
a mass of smaller inner petals
in the traditional quartered
style of the Old Rose. The
colour is a dusky lilac-pink,
which appears as a cool lilac
in subdued light – a colour
much used by the Scottish
Art Nouveau designer after
whom the rose is named.

H 1m (3½ft) × W 90cm (3ft) 1988

charlotte

Charlotte is one of my favourite roses. With its soft yellow colouring and beautifully arranged, deeply cupped blooms, it is quite simply a superb rose. A smaller, more feminine version of the very popular Graham Thomas from which it was bred, it shares the same delicate Tea Rose scent that is prevalent among yellow English Roses. The flowers are nicely poised on a bushy shrub, and are borne with great freedom throughout the summer.

H 1m (3½ft) x W 75cm (2½ft) 1993

chianti

The founding red English Rose, introduced in 1967,
'Chianti' is a cross between the repeat- and summer-
flowering Gallica 'Tuscany' and Floribunda 'Dusky Maiden'.
It is a vigorous, large and shapely shrub, the red
counterpart of Constance Spry. Although
it only flowers once, the fine blooms
are worthy of comparison with the
very best of the Old Roses, and
the wealth of large, crimson-purple
Gallica-like flowers form a dramatic
display, even as they are fading
to a rich purple. Old Rose
in appearance, being rosette-shaped
and with many petals, the flowers also
have a powerful Old Rose fragrance
which adds to their attraction.

H 1.5m (5ft) x W 1.5m (5ft) 1967

claire rose

At their best, the blooms of Claire Rose are large, magnificent and often of superb quality. The large and strongly fragrant flowers are a delicate blush-pink at first – although they do fade with age – and they open very gradually to form a flat rosette, before eventually recurving slightly. The growth is unusually vigorous and upright, and the large, modern-type leaves and vigorous habit are much like Charles Austin, from which it is directly descended. Nevertheless, it can appear ungainly, so it is best planted at the back of a border behind other plants, or grouped with two companions. This rose has proved a little disappointing in Britain as its flowers 'spottle' in rain. In warmer climates, I would expect no such problem.

H 1.2m (4ft) x W 1m (3½ft) 1986

bright crimson

l.d. braithwaite   *among late-summer*

hips and *blackberrieas*

constance spry

Introduced in 1961, Constance Spry is the original English Rose. As the offspring of Gallica 'Belle Isis' and the repeat-flowering Floribunda 'Dusky Maiden', it flowers only once during the summer, but when it does there are few finer sights among roses. It can be grown as a vigorous shrub which may require some support or, perhaps, as a superb climber. The soft pink flowers are large and sump-tuous, with a strong spicy fragrance, redolent of myrrh.

H 1.8m (6ft) x W 1.8m (6ft) 1961

cottage rose

True to its name, this is an
ideal rose for the smaller or
less formal garden, where its
charming flowers of loose
rosette shape with a 'button
eye', its rather narrow upright
habit and its ability to produce
blooms with remarkable
continuity throughout the
summer will make it the
perfect choice. An added
bonus is the delicate Old Rose
fragrance with a suggestion of
white lilac. The blooms are
medium-sized, shallow-cupped
rosettes in pure, glowing pink.

H 1m (3½ft) x W 75cm (2½ft) 1991

country living

Country Living is in many ways the epitome of the English Rose – in the perfect Old Rose configuration of the full-petalled, quartered blooms with their green 'button eye'; in the lovely soft blush-pink colour; and in the compact, well-balanced habit of growth. It is a delicate, fragrant rose that requires tender loving care if it is to show its true potential. Plant it at the front of a border where you can appreciate its charms to the full.

H 90cm (3ft) x W 60cm (2ft) 1991

dr. herbert gray

This is a captivating little rose, with clear pink, cupped flowers of perfect formation like carved sea shells above foliage with a blue-grey tinge. Its free-flowering nature makes it ideal as a bedding rose, though it would be equally at home at the front of the rose border. It has a Damask fragrance with an aniseed note. This lovely rose was named after the founder of the British charity Relate, to commemorate their Diamond Jubilee.

H 75cm (2½ft) x W 60cm (2ft) 1998

eglantyne

For me, this is perhaps the most charming English Rose. The flowers are of rosette formation, with numerous small petals arranged in perfect symmetry. Named after Eglantyne Jebb, who founded the Save the Children Fund during World War 1, the flowers are saucer-shaped, with the petals turning up a little at the edges. The colour is a soft pink and there is a delicious fragrance. Moreover, the rose suffers little from disease.

H 1m (3½ft) x H 75cm (2½ft) 1994

emily

To watch one of these blooms unfold is a unique experience. At first there is a dainty little cup of pale shell-pink petals; then the outer petals open flat, leaving the inner petals still cupped until the inner petals open to form a perfect rosette shape; finally, the outer petals reflex still further in a fourth beautiful transformation. Emily is not very vigorous and is difficult to grow well, but will repay your devotion with some of the most exquisite flowers.

H 75cm (2½ft) x W 60cm (2ft) 1992

english elegance

The subtle coloration of English Elegance combines many different shades of pink, salmon and copper, fading to a paler pink at the outer edges. This makes it an ideal rose for mingling with other plants. Alternatively, place it at the back of a rose border where its tall, graceful growth can arch over and through that of its neighbours, holding its large blooms aloft. This is a lovely large shrub with huge flowers that is truly worthy of its name.

H 1.5m (5ft) x W 1.2m (4ft) 1986

english garden

English Garden's rather short, upright growth makes it an excellent substitute for the Hybrid Tea as a bedding rose, with the additional bonus of beautiful, flat, full-petalled flowers of perfect Old Rose formation. The blooms are soft yellow at the centre, tending almost to white on the outer petals, and are set above fresh, pale green foliage. A bed of these roses would grace any garden! The flowers have a light Tea Rose fragrance.

H 1m (3½ft) x W 75cm (2½ft) 1986

the loose-petalled

blooms of mary rose

display an *old rose charm*

evelyn

Evelyn has, perhaps, the most luscious scent of all the English Roses. It is similar to the classic Old Rose fragrance, but has a fruity note reminiscent of peaches and apricots. The fragrance was chosen by perfumiers Crabtree & Evelyn for their rose perfume. The blooms look as good as they smell: the centre of each flower is a mixture of apricot and yellow quartered petals with a hint of pink, held in a curving bowl of paler outer petals.

H 1m (3½ft) x W 75cm (2½ft) 1991

fair bianca

As beautiful as its namesake,
Shakespeare's character,
this small white rose is not
quite as good-tempered as
the fictional Bianca, having
numerous small thorns! But it
has some of the most perfect
flowers of all the English Roses
– fully double rosettes with
just a hint of cream at the
base. Dark pink in the closed
bud, Fair Bianca has light
green foliage and the rich
Old Rose fragrance of the
classic Alba Roses, with a
haunting note of heliotrope.

H 90cm (3ft) x W 60cm (2ft) 1982

francine austin

This is not strictly an English Rose, but a ground-cover rose. It is, however, the offspring of an Old Noisette Rose, which makes it rather different. The dainty clusters of white pompom flowers – pink in bud – tumble about the rose border, setting off the other flowers. With its arching growth, it is a versatile rose: use it as ground cover, to edge the front of a border, or further back in the border where it will mix in with the other roses.

H 1m (3⅓ft) x W 1.2m (4ft) 1988

gertrude jekyll

A magnificent rose and a
fitting tribute to Britain's
greatest woman gardener,
Gertrude Jekyll has large,
rich pink flowers and a
well-balanced, Old Rose
perfume, described as the
quintessential rose fragrance.
Its breeding includes the
Old Portland Rose, Comte
de Chambord, with which
it shares its scent and strong
growth as well as an ability to
produce flowers well into the
autumn. The flowers open to
shapely well-filled rosettes.

H 1.2m (4ft) x W 1m (3½ft) 1986

glamis castle

Producing a light, airy effect when planted *en masse*, the white Glamis Castle is equally at home at the front of the border, in the small garden or in rose beds, where its bushy growth makes it an ideal choice. This outstanding rose has all the charm of an Old Rose, coupled with an ability to flower right through the season with all the freedom of a Floribunda. Glamis Castle has an intriguing myrrh-like fragrance.

H 1m (3½ft) x W 75cm (2½ft) 1992

*golden
celebration*

Enormous, incurving flowers
of splendid copper-yellow —
unique even among the many
yellow English Roses — are
well balanced by the strong,
elegantly arching stems
on which they are borne.
Although very large in flower,
with a strong, fruity fragrance,
it is perfectly balanced in
all its parts. It is remarkably
resistant to disease, and is
an excellent and reliable
all-round rose that combines
beauty with easy maintenance.

H 1.2m (4ft) x W 1.2m (4ft) 1992

graham thomas

With its vibrant, clear yellow colouring, shapely blooms, vigorous yet elegant growth and free-flowering habit, this versatile and reliable rose amply deserves the popularity it has held since it was introduced in 1983. It can be grown either as a shrub or as a short climber. An excellent rose in every way, we are proud that it was chosen by Graham Stuart Thomas, the great rose expert, to bear his name. It has a fresh Tea Rose fragrance.

H 1.2m (4ft) x W 1.2m (4ft) 1983

happy child

The deep sunshine-yellow of
Happy Child is unique among
English Roses, as are the
leaves, which are thick and
highly polished like a camellia.
But this medium-sized shrub
shows itself to be a true
English Rose in its
graceful, slightly
arching growth, and in
the characteristic Old Rose
shape of the flowers. This rose
is useful wherever a deep
yellow accent is desired. It has
a light Old Rose fragrance
with a touch of lemon.

H 1.2m (4ft) x W 1m (3½ft) 1993

nor will in fading silks compose

faintly the inimitable rose

ANNE FINCH, LADY WINCHILSEA

One of Clay Perry's most beautiful rose photographs, depicting Glamis Castle, Evelyn and Redouté

heather austin

A large, chalice-shaped bloom with slightly incurved petals that open to reveal the yellow stamens within. The colour is a deep, rich pink and the whole flower has a definite Old Rose character. It also has a strong and delicious Old Rose fragrance. The growth is vigorous and bushy and it is generally free from disease. Although rather tall for some gardens, it is useful at the back of a border. This rose was named after my sister.

H 1.2m (4ft) × W 1m (3½ft) 1996

heritage

This superb variety is
deservedly one of the most
popular English Roses, with
clear shell-pink flowers
poised above a shapely,
well-rounded bush. It has a
warm fragrance, a mixture of
honey and clove-carnation.
The blooms are of perfect
cupped formation, with the
outer petals paling from
blush-pink to almost white,
enclosing row upon row of
pink inner petals. The flowers
are borne with great freedom
throughout the summer.

H 1.2m (4ft) x W 1.2m (4ft) 1984

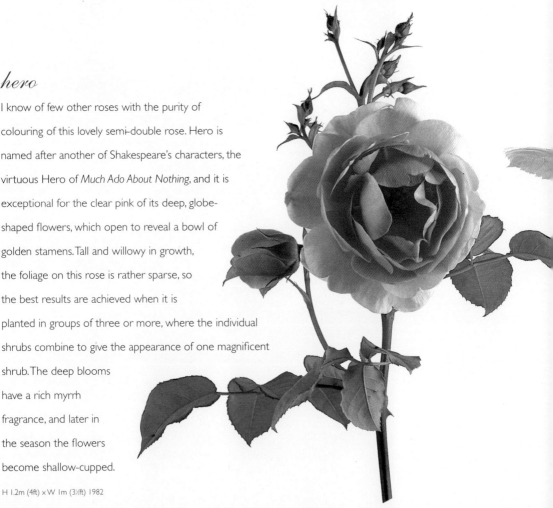

hero

I know of few other roses with the purity of colouring of this lovely semi-double rose. Hero is named after another of Shakespeare's characters, the virtuous Hero of *Much Ado About Nothing*, and it is exceptional for the clear pink of its deep, globe-shaped flowers, which open to reveal a bowl of golden stamens. Tall and willowy in growth, the foliage on this rose is rather sparse, so the best results are achieved when it is planted in groups of three or more, where the individual shrubs combine to give the appearance of one magnificent shrub. The deep blooms have a rich myrrh fragrance, and later in the season the flowers become shallow-cupped.

H 1.2m (4ft) x W 1m (3½ft) 1982

jayne austin

A rose of great charm and refinement, Jayne Austin is
descended from the famous climbing Old Rose,
'Gloire de Dijon', from which it inherits
the silky, luminous texture of its
petals and their colouring
of soft yellow, tending
a little towards apricot.
The flowers are of a
beautiful rosette
formation, and are
carried on a dense, robust bush with plentiful, pale green
foliage. It can tend towards ungainliness, but careful pruning of
the many long shoots will maintain a good overall shape. Named
after my daughter-in-law, Jayne Austin has a delicate, fresh
Tea Rose fragrance with a hint of lilac. It can
be affected by harsh weather conditions.

H 1.2m (4ft) x W 75cm (2½ft) 1990

john clare

Profusion is a great
virtue in a rose, and
John Clare is the most
generous of roses, providing
an abundance of flowers
right through the summer
and on into the autumn,
when its wonderful display
is particularly welcome. The
medium-sized, light crimson
blooms are simpler and
more informal than many
English Roses, as befits
a rose dedicated to the
memory of the countryside
poet, John Clare.

H 1m (3½ft) x W 75cm (2½ft) 1994

jude the obscure

Like the hero of Thomas Hardy's novel, after whom it is named, this rose can be temperamental. It has a healthy constitution but, like some famous roses of the past (such as 'Souvenir de la Malmaison'), its incurving, cupped, golden blooms sometimes fail to open in very wet weather. However, in a reasonably dry summer, this rose will produce some of the best flowers of any rose that I know. It is, therefore, well suited to dry climates.

H 1m (3½ft) x W 1.2m (4ft) 1995

kathryn morley

Named by Mr and Mrs Eric Morley of the Variety Club in memory of their daughter, this rose is one of my favourites. The soft pink flowers, gracefully held on tall stems, are beautifully shaped with a refinement that is unusual in blooms of this size. The broad outer petals enclose a bowl of smaller notched and frilled petals with something of the effect of a Japanese paeony. Its delicate fragrance is an elegiac blend of Old Rose and myrrh.

H 1.5m (5ft) × W 1m (3½ft) 1990

l.d. braithwaite

L.D. Braithwaite is that
most useful of roses: a
good unfading red with the
ability to produce flower
throughout the season. It
has informal, loose-petalled
blooms, which open to reveal
the occasional golden stamen
in the flower's velvety heart.
It is the perfect choice when
a bright crimson is wanted
for the rose bed; alternatively
it can act as an exclamation
mark in an otherwise pastel
border. It has a good
Old Rose fragrance.

H 1.2m (4ft) x W 1m (3½ft) 1988

what is fairer than a rose?

what is sweeter?

GEORGE HERBERT

Evelyn, one of the most fragrant of all roses, used by Crabtree & Evelyn for their rose perfume

leander

Leander bears large, open sprays of small, deep apricot flowers – smaller versions of those of its parent, Charles Austin. The two roses also share the same shiny, dark foliage. But there the similarity ends, for Leander is a large, bushy, disease-resistant shrub or climber. It also has a rich fruity fragrance with a delightful hint of raspberries. It is summer-flowering, and occasionally blooms again in autumn. In warm climates it repeats more continuously.

H 1.8m (6ft) × 150cm (5ft) 1982

lilac rose

As its name suggests, the blooms of this rose are a delicate lilac colour. The soft, many-petalled rosettes have an exceptionally strong fragrance. The shrub itself is short and bushy, but rather flat-topped. It is at its best planted towards the front of the border with other roses, for it lends depth and harmony to neighbouring colours. It can also be used like a Modern Hybrid Tea, as a bedding rose, in a formal quasi-Edwardian rose bed.

W 75cm (2½ft) x H 90cm (3ft)

lilian austin

I love to see this rose at the front of a border where, with its low, spreading habit, it softens the edges of a lawn or path, and its fragrance wafts into the air as you brush past. The colour is salmon-pink with orange and apricot tints. Wide, loosely formed, semi-double flowers are produced continually throughout the summer. Named after my flower-loving mother, Lilian Austin has played a crucial role in the development of English Roses.

H 1.5m (5ft) x W 1.2m (4ft) 1973

marinette

In full bloom this lovely shrub looks just as if it were covered with butterflies. The long, slender buds open to delicate, cream and pink, semi-double flowers, which at first are pointed at the centre, a little like a Hybrid Tea, but then open wide and flat to reveal soft pink petals with creamy-yellow hearts and golden stamens. The whole effect is wonderfully light and airy. Use it to set off the heavier flowers of the more typical English Roses.

H 1.5m (5ft) x W 1.2m (4ft) 1995

mary magdalene

The exceptionally beautiful blooms of this rose, named after our local church, have a true Old Rose character. They open rather flat and quartered with a 'button eye', and the smaller inner petals are slightly notched and frilled giving them a charm that is hard to capture in a photograph. There is a delicious rose fragrance, with just a touch of aniseed. The growth tends to be broad, with the branches spreading out at an angle.

H 1m (3½ft) x W 1m (3½ft) 1998

mary rose

Introduced in 1983 to great acclaim, Mary Rose is still one of the most widely planted of all English Roses. It is one of the first English Roses to flower and it continues to do so intermittently until well into the autumn. The flowers are a warm pink and have a light fragrance. It is an excellent, disease-resistant shrub with well-tempered growth – characteristics that have recommended it as the parent of many of our best recent roses.

H 1.2m (4ft) x W 1.2m (4ft) 1983

mistress quickly

The offspring of a Noisette–Rugosa cross, this rose is tough and reliable, and it also seems to be entirely free of disease. The growth is upright, the foliage is dark greyish-green, and the clusters of lightly scented, pink flowers are small for an English Rose — no larger than those of a typical rambler. Mistress Quickly is ideal for a mixed border, where its continuous display of flowers will be held above smaller plants to create a very pleasing effect.

H 1.2m (4ft) x W 1m (3½ft) 1995

molineux

With its rich golden flowers,
Molineux is ideal for massed
planting in rose beds, where
its short, upright growth,
good disease resistance and
continuity of flowering make
it a good substitute for Hybrid
Teas or Floribundas. Although
it is not a typical English
Rose, there are few roses
that are as reliable. At the
Royal National Rose Society's
1996 trials, Molineux won a
Gold Medal as well as the
Henry Edland medal for
the Best Scented Rose.

H 1m (3½ft) × W 75cm (2½ft) 1995

purple veronica

*is the **perfect** foil for*

kathryn morley's soft pink

mrs doreen pike

The soft pink, Old Rose flowers of
this rose contrast well with the
pale green, Rugosa-like foliage.
Add a near-perfect, mound-like
habit of growth, and the result
is an extremely good garden
shrub. The flowers – while very
beautiful at their
best – do not always
form well late in the
summer, and sometimes
fail to open in damp weather. An extremely
reliable shrub, it will grow anywhere, although a
little fertilizer will produce better flowers. There is a
lovely Old Rose fragrance. This rose was named
after the long-time manageress of our office.

H 1m (3½ft) x W 1.2m (4ft) 1993

noble antony

This rose has short, bushy growth and the flowers are a little different to other English Roses, with petals that turn down to create a perfectly domed formation – a feature that does not show up in the photograph, which was taken at the half-open stage. The colour of the blooms is bright crimson at first, becoming a pleasing shade of deep magenta-crimson. They have a very rich, well-balanced Old Rose fragrance.

H 1m (3½ft) x W 75cm (2½ft) 1995

pat austin

Although this rose's growth resembles that of its pollen parent Abraham Darby, the colour of its large, cupped flowers may seem surprisingly strong, particularly to those aware of our endeavours to encourage softer, purer shades. The inside of the petals is a bright copper, while the outside is a pale copper-yellow, making this rose the ideal choice for brightening up a border of pastels. The unique fragrance has a hint of carnation.

H 1.2m (4ft) x W 1m (3½ft) 1995

pegasus

This is a graceful rose with the flowers held elegantly on arching branches, making it perfect for flower arrangements. Both the flowers and the foliage have something of the character of a camellia, the leaves being quite dark and polished in appearance. The waxy petals are a rich, apricot-yellow colour, fading almost to cream at the edges of the flower. They also carry a pleasing Tea Rose fragrance.

H 1m (3½ft) x W 1m (3½ft) 1995

perdita

Named after the lost
daughter in Shakespeare's
play *The Winter's Tale*, this
rose has an unusual fragrance
with a complex hint of spice,
not unlike a nicotiana. The
quartered blooms are an
apricot-blush: at first soft
pink at the centre with
almost white edges, they later
become blush-pink flushed
with yellow at the base of
the petals. It was awarded
the Henry Edland Medal for
fragrance at the National
Rose Society's trials in 1984.

H 1m (3½ft) x W 75cm (2½ft) 1983

prospero

Worth growing for its deep and fruity Old Rose fragrance alone, Prospero also has beautiful, rich, dark crimson flowers like the best of the old Gallica Roses. The blooms are composed of numerous small petals arranged with perfect symmetry into domed rosettes. Although it is not very robust, and is not an easy rose to grow, when its scent fills the air on a midsummer's night you too will fall under the enchanter's spell.

H 75cm (2½ft) × W 60cm (2ft) 1982

radio times

Radio Times bears perfect, slightly dome-shaped blooms on a small, neat, arching bush. The flowers are a lovely, fresh, clear pink with a strong Old Rose fragrance, and the petals tend to curve back as the flower grows older. The shrub is seen to best effect when planted in groups of three or more. This is a beautiful little rose, but it does have a slight tendency to suffer blackspot in areas where disease is prevalent.

H 1m (3½ft) × W 75cm (2½ft) 1994

redouté

A delicate silvery-pink sport of the much-loved Mary Rose, with all the good qualities of its parent and – if at all possible – even more beautiful. It is free-flowering, with the same honey fragrance and exceptional resistance to disease. Redouté is named after the most famous rose painter, Pierre-Joseph Redouté (1759–1840), whose watercolours of the Empress Josephine's roses at Malmaison represent for many people the epitome of the Old Rose. It is one of the first English Roses to flower and it repeats continually thereafter until the onset of winter.

H 1m (3½ft) × W 1m (3½ft) 1992

a lovely being, scarcely

form'd or moulded,

a rose with all its sweetest

leaves yet folded

LORD BYRON

Sunlight shining through a bowl of English Roses, including Golden Celebration, The Alexandra Rose and Evelyn

st cecilia

In apparent contradiction, this short-growing rose is characterized by elegance and poise, making it an attractive choice for a garden with little room for expansive gestures. Widely spaced in open sprays, the cupped flowers, bearing a strong myrrh fragrance, bend forward on slightly arching stems, their subtle colouring changing from pale buff-apricot to almost white. The foliage is rather scarce, which only seems to enhance the beauty of the blooms.

H 1m (3½ft) x W 75cm (2½ft) 1987

st swithun

A rather taller-than-usual
English Rose, which is
perhaps better planted in a
group of two or three to
form a tangled mass. Its
flowers are large and rosette-
shaped, turning up at the
edges. The colour is a delicate
blush-pink, giving a charming,
soft effect. There is a fruity,
myrrh fragrance with a hint
of aniseed. This rose was
named after St Swithun,
the founder of Winchester
Cathedral, in celebration of
its 900th anniversary.

H 1.5m (5ft) x W 1m (3½ft) 1993

scepter'd isle

A pretty little rose, bearing
quite small, cup-shaped
flowers in great profusion;
perhaps more plentifully
than any other English
Rose. The colour is a
soft pink, paling towards the
outer petals with a boss of
golden stamens just visible
within. The growth is upright,
with flowers held above the
foliage. There is a strong myrrh
fragrance. An ideal rose for
a very small garden, it is also
suitable for bedding, in the
manner of a Hybrid Tea.

H 1m (3½ft) x W 75cm (2½ft) 1996

sharifa asma

The flower of Sharifa Asma is
the quintessence of all that
an Old Rose should be. Its
shallow cup of pink incurving
petals reflexes at the top
to form a perfect
rosette, with paler,
almost white outer
petals, and just a suggestion
of a 'button eye'. It has the
translucent quality of mother-
of-pearl, and it should be
planted where it will not be
damaged by hot sun. Sharifa
Asma has a distinctive scent
with a hint of mulberries.

H 1.2m (4ft) x W 1m (3½ft) 1983

sir edward elgar

Just as the great composer himself stood
out among contemporary musicians,
so the flowers of 'Sir Edward Elgar'
make it unusual among red roses. Set
against fairly dark green foliage, the colours
of the flowers can vary greatly between cerise and
crimson according to the whims of the weather, looking
their most attractive on a hot, sunny summer's day.
Blooms are initially cupped but later recurve to become
neatly domed. Characteristically for
an 'Aloha' descendant, the bush is
upright, but its growth is
somewhat less vigorous
than one usually finds
in other roses of
the same strain.

H 1m (3½ft) x W 75cm (2½ft) 1992

sweet juliet

Sweet Juliet has flowers
of a pleasing rosette
formation. Dainty buds
open to reveal a small
'button eye', and the blooms vary in
colour from a deep apricot at the centre to
a ring of paler petals around the outside.
The flowers also have a pleasant fresh
fragrance with a hint of orange blossom.
It is a tall and vigorous shrub of
upright habit, and it produces an
abundance of disease-free foliage.
In fact, it is such a vigorous rose that
at times it makes growth at the expense
of flowers: quite severe pruning and thinning
are, therefore, recommended.

H 1.2m (4ft) x W 1m (3½ft) 1989

teasing georgia

Teasing Georgia has flowers of unusual formation and colour: the centre petals are in the form of a deep yellow cup, while the outer petals fall back and fade to palest yellow, creating a two-tone effect. The growth is strong but graceful, and it will form a substantial bush with good, disease-resistant foliage. It repeats well and there is a fresh Tea Rose fragrance. It was named for Mr Ulrich Meyer after his wife, Georgia.

H 1m (3½ft) × 1m (3½ft) 1998

tess of the d'urbervilles

The passionate nature of Thomas Hardy's Tess is perfectly captured in the vibrant colouring of this crimson rose. Deeply cupped in the early stages, the flowers open with a gentle informality, inclining their heads in a manner that has great charm. The petals reflex slightly as they open, releasing their Old Rose fragrance into the air. The vibrant colour is complemented by dark foliage, on a robust and spreading bush.

H 1m (3½ft) x W 1m (3½ft) 1998

change in a trice
the lilies and languors of virtue
for the raptures and roses of vice

ALGERNON CHARLES SWINBURNE

The spray rose Francine Austin helps to lighten the rather heavy effect of other English Roses

the countryman

This is one of my favourite roses and a back-cross to an Old Portland Rose; the flowers are of the clearest rose-pink imaginable, with narrow, quilted petals opening to form a perfect rosette. The growth is usually upright at first; the branches eventually fall to form a low, spreading shrub, with the long, slender leaves of a Damask Rose. The Countryman has a powerful and delicious Old Rose fragrance.

H 90cm (3ft) x W 1m (3½ft) 1987

the dark lady

As beautiful and enigmatic as the dark lady of Shakespeare's sonnets, this broad, spreading rose has a strong Old Rose fragrance. The large, dusky crimson blooms are set against rich dark green foliage. The petals open flat and then recurve a little, displaying an informal character reminiscent of the tree paeony found in Chinese fabric design. The growth of the shrub is strong but not excessive, being proportionate to the bold character of the bloom.

H 1m (3½ft) x W 1m (3½ft) 1991

the herbalist

The historical overtones of The Herbalist's name are particularly appropriate, given the similarity of its blooms to those of the Apothecary's Rose, *R. gallica* var. *officinalis*. It flowers freely and inter-mittently throughout the summer, and the semi-double blooms of deep pink or light crimson open flat, exposing golden stamens. Modest and unassuming, this rose is ideal for a mixed border, while its compact growth makes it suitable for a low hedge.

H 90cm (3ft) × W 90cm (3ft) 1991

the pilgrim

This is one of the most reliable and beautiful of the yellow English Roses. Softer in both colour and texture than its parent plant Graham Thomas, the silky flowers of The Pilgrim are made up of a multitude of small yellow petals arranged in a perfect rosette shape. It is a robust rose, growing and flowering freely, and it has a light myrrh fragrance. For some gardens, it may be a little too tall, but it is ideal at the back of a border.

H 1m (3½ft) x W 90cm (3ft) 1991

the prince

The Prince is a rose of
superb colouring, unique
among Modern Roses. The
fragrant blooms open as the
deepest, richest crimson
imaginable and quickly turn
to a magnificent and equally
rich dark violet-purple,
reminiscent of the best old
Gallicas. The glossy, dark
foliage and low, spreading
habit make it particularly
suitable for the front of a
border, where its powerful
Old Rose fragrance can be
appreciated to the full.

H 75cm (2½ ft) × W 60cm (2ft) 1990

the reeve

Named after one of Chaucer's pilgrims from *The Canterbury Tales*, The Reeve descends from Chaucer, one of my earliest roses. The dusky pink, globular blooms are set above dark, matt leaves, and incurving petals open to reveal golden stamens within. The flowers have a strong Old Rose fragrance, and the thorny stems give this rose a graceful, arching growth. The subtlety of The Reeve will appeal to the most discerning eye.

H 1.2m (4ft) × W 1.2m (4ft) 1979

tradescant

This wine-dark rose recalls the velvety texture and deep colour of the old Gallica Rose 'Tuscany', but it has the additional advantage of being repeat-flowering. The full-petalled, quartered blooms are set on a short, arching bush — like most dark roses. The powerful Damask fragrance has a refreshing sharpness. This rose is named in honour of the two John Tradescants, 17th-century gardeners and plant collectors.

H 1m (3½ft) x W 75cm (2½ft) 1993

trevor griffiths

This rose has much of
the Old Rose character.
The flowers are dusky pink
with paler outer petals, and
they open flat. The bush
tends to be rather short, with
branches growing out-wards
to form a nice bushy shrub.
The leaves are dusky green
and they complement the
flowers to create a charming
overall effect. This rose
is named after my friend
Trevor Griffiths, New
Zealand's leading specialist
in Old and English Roses.

H 1m (3½ft) x W 90cm (3ft) 1994

tis the last rose of summer

left blooming alone;

all her lovely companions

are faded and gone

THOMAS MOORE

A casual arrangement of English Roses in a pewter jug. Note how well the soft colours blend

wenlock

This rose combines rich crimson colouring, fragrance and vigour. The flowers are large and in some respects they lack the quality of other red English Roses. It is, however, a reliable rose. The flowers are shallowly cupped, paling a little with age, and they repeat throughout the season. The rich Old Rose fragrance has a sharp, citrus note. This rose is named after Much Wenlock, a medieval town near our nursery.

H 1.2m (4ft) x W 1m (3½ft)

william morris

William Morris is a tall, vigorous shrub with graceful, arching growth. Held above glossy foliage, the glowing apricot-pink blooms are filled with quartered petals in a formal rosette shape. This rose has good repeat-flowering qualities and good disease resistance, as well as a fresh fragrance with a cool note of cucumber. It is named after the 19th-century artist, designer and political thinker, to mark the centenary of the University of East London.

H 1.2m (4ft) × W 1m (3½ft) 1998

winchester cathedral

This is a lovely sport of the famous Mary Rose. Winchester Cathedral possesses all the virtues of its parent, which it resembles in every way except for its colour, being white with an occasional tinge of yellow later in the year. It has excellent, vigorous growth and good repeat-flowering properties, and it is just as reliable as Mary Rose. The light Old Rose fragrance has a hint of honey.

H 1.2m (4ft) x W 1.2m (4ft)

windflower

Windflower is quite unusual among English Roses. The flowers are cup-shaped with few petals and stand above the foliage in the manner of a herbaceous anemone. The effect is one of daintiness and charm, and this is complemented by the fresh, myrrh-like fragrance. In addition, it is an unusually healthy bush. On one side, it is descended from the Alba Roses, which are themselves descended from the dog rose of hedgerows.

H 90cm (3ft) x W 1.2m (4ft) 1994

suppliers

English Roses are also available at leading garden centres in all countries.

Australia

The Flower Garden
Shakes Road, Nairne 5252

The Perfumed Garden
47 Rendlesham Avenue
Mt. Eliza, Victoria 3930

Melville Nurseries Pty. Ltd.
40 Mason Hill Road
Carmel, Perth 6076

Swane Bros. Pty. Ltd.
490 Galston Road
P.O. Box 29, Dural
NSW 2158

Belgium

Boomkwekerijen
LOUIS LENS NV,
Redinnestraat 11
B8460 Oudenburg

Canada

Old Rose Nursery
Central Road, Hornby Island
British Columbia V0R 1Z0

Pickering Nurseries Inc.
670 Kingston Road
Pickering, Ontario L1V 1A6

V. Kraus Nurseries Ltd.
Carlisle, Ontario L0R 1H0

Denmark

Assens Planteskole
Faaborgvej 10–12
DK–5610 Assens

France

Georges Delbard SA
16 Quai de la Megisserie
75054 Paris

Germany

Ingwer J Jensen GMBH
Am Schlosspark 2B
24960 Glücksburg

Greece

Panos Avramis & Sons OE
Agathovoulou 10
581 00 Giannitsa

Holland

Rozenkwekerij De Wilde
Postbus 15
1400 AC Bussum

Italy

Rose Barni
Via Autostrada 5
51100 Pistoia

Japan

Rose of Roses, Ltd.
87, 2-Chome
Sujikai Kitagata-cho
Motosu-Gun, Gifu Pref.

New Zealand

Bob Matthews Nursery
P.O. Box 574
Wanganui

Egmont Roses
P.O. Box 3162
New Plymouth

Trevor Griffiths Roses Ltd.
No. 3 RD, Timaru

South Africa

Ludwigs Roses
P.O. Box 28165
0132 Sunnyside, Pretoria

Switzerland

Richard Huber AG
5605 Dottikon

United Kingdom

David Austin Roses Ltd.
Bowling Green Lane
Albrighton
Wolverhampton WV7 3HB

USA

Arena Rose Company
1524 Via Rosa
Paso Robles
California 93446

Heirloom Old Garden Roses
24062 NE Riverside Drive
St. Paul, Oregon 97137

Jackson & Perkins Ltd.
P.O. Box 1028
2518 South Pacific Highway
Medford, Oregon 97501

Wayside Gardens
Geo. W. Park Seed Co. Inc.
Cokesbury Road
Greenwood
South Carolina 29647–0001

Acknowledgements

The Publishers would like to thank the following photographers and organizations for their kind permission to reproduce the following photographs in this book:

Clay Perry: 4–5, 6, 8, 10, 12, 13, 14, 16, 17, 18, 19, 20–21, 22, 23, 26, 27, 30–31, 32, 33, 35, 36, 37, 39, 41, 43, 44, 45, 46, 49, 51, 52, 54, 55, 57, 60–61, 62, 63, 64, 65, 66, 68, 69, 71, 72, 73, 75, 76, 77, 81, 82, 83, 85, 88, 89, 91, 95

John Glover, Vincent Page and Howard Rice for David Austin Roses: 2, 9, 15, 24, 25, 28, 29, 34, 38, 42, 47, 48, 53, 56, 58, 59, 67, 74, 78, 79, 84, 86, 87, 92, 93, 94

John Glover: 47